REGIME OF CONVENTION

REGIME OF CONVENTION

✦

The Swiss Case

Adolfo Mazariegos

iUniverse, Inc.
New York Lincoln Shanghai

REGIME OF CONVENTION
The Swiss Case

iUniverse books may be ordered through booksellers or by contacting:

iUniverse
2021 Pine Lake Road, Suite 100
Lincoln, NE 68512
www.iuniverse.com
1-800-Authors (1-800-288-4677)

Original title: Régimen de Convención, El caso suizo.
Translation: Roberto Quezada
Additional translation: Adolfo Mazariegos
Translation from Spanish, ©2005 by Adolfo Mazariegos

ISBN: 0-595-34783-5

Printed in the United States of America

Contents

INTRODUCTION

The Regime of Convention is the governmental system that for a long time has characterized the Helvetian Confederation (Switzerland). Notwithstanding its importance in the context of government theories—given that as a theory it is much more ancient than parliamentarism or presidentialism—[1]when seeking information on this topic, such search turns out to be fruitless most of the times (except, of course, in treaties that result being extensive or complicated for someone tyro in this topic). This happens often to students of political sciences and/or related careers, who stumble into difficulties in finding a simple way, therefore making it easy to analyze the topic at hand.

When students begin a university career, usually (and it is to a larger extent logical), due to their superior instruction, they look into texts in whose pages they can find, in an accessible manner, basic information regarding theories that may help them find a gradual introduction into a world of knowledge inherent to a certain discipline, such being the case known as Regime of Convention (or Conventional Regime).

Nowadays this system, as a government theory brought into practice, has to be analyzed beginning with the fact that government theories, as they are known, have a support that undoubtedly is linked to the history and political evolution of the states (keeping in mind that not all states develop at the same rhythm and with the same trends) since government structures—which evidently include their political institutions—answer in great part to the needs,

---

1. Parliamentarism and presidentialism are theories that developed in the XVIII century. (See: Douglas V. Verney, *Analysis of the Political Systems*. Editorial Tecnos, Buenos Aires, Argentina, page 63).

changes, and even popular demands produced throughout their history.

Maurice Duverger points out that *the political institutions are linked to the economic-social structures, to the levels of development, to the ideologies and value systems, and to cultural traditions.*[2] Douglas V. Verney indicates that *in the heart of any government system, there are certain notions that can be designed as their own theory. The word theory, however, can be somehow deceptive, because it means to some people that men have thought out first how a government must be led, and then have devoted themselves to putting into practice its principles.*[3] This asseveration made by Verney is sufficiently precise as far as the topic it illustrates is concerned, but it seems not to be applicable to the concrete case of Switzerland (country whose case is presented in this research). In other words, the term theory—as it has been used—does not produce the same deceptive effect if a previous review is made of the history of the Helvetian Confederation, because only then a great portion of the notions taken as reference, turn out to be the product of demands from this particular democratic tradition (direct democracy, or semi-direct, or municipal autonomy) whose results have been obtained practically during its own historical development and in its conformation as a union of states.

As it is delved deeply into these topics, it is understood that they cannot and must not be taken lightly, and that it would be a mistake to try to understand a theory of so much importance by making a

---

2.   Maurice Duverger. *Political Institutions and Constitutional Law (Preface)*. Editions Ariel, S.A. Spain, 1970. Page 7.
3.   Douglas V. Verney, Op. Cit.

superficial analysis of it, both because of its importance and because of the objectivity with which it must be approached; at the same time this explains the scarcity of short articles that can describe and deal with this topic.

The research presented here has been carried out thinking in terms of facilitating in some manner the search to the interested readers, but especially as a desire to assist the students that just begin their first steps into the social sciences (particularly political sciences and international relations), offering a warning that this is only an introduction to a conventional theory carried out to practice, by means of a description of a concrete case regarding the structure of a conventional government and its distribution of powers. Let us hope these lines may become easy and understandable reading, through an uncomplicated panoramic view of the subject hereby presented; it should be emphasized that the scientific knowledge must be deep and, of course, objective.

1

THE SWISS CONFEDERATION

1.1. HISTORIC REVIEW

The history of the Swiss Confederation is very important, above all if it is considered that it is unavoidably linked to the general history of Europe. We could easily go back to the era of the Helvetians, the *Recios,* and the Romans circa year 107 B.C., or the epoch of the *Burgundios* and the *Alamanos*, which is the stage that brought a pronounced division of the languages, including the years 2000 to 3000 B.C., time in which the lands of the current Swiss territory were already being tilled. As a matter of fact, Switzerland is known by many as *the oldest country or republic in the world.*

However, even in our era, the year 1291 acquires special importance in the Swiss history, since in that year takes place the first pact[1] among the *waldstaetten*[2] from Uri, Schwyz and Unterwalden[3]. In the hidden prairies of *Rütli*, representatives of the free peasants from those cantons founded a confederation known as *Everlasting League* and swore to help one another, especially in order to rid themselves from the servitude imposed upon them by the Habsburgs.[4]

---

1. Traditionally, it is said in Switzerland that the oath, reason for the pact, took place on August 1, 1291. (See: Pierre Cordey, *Encounter With Switzerland—The Historic Evolution.* OSEC. Switzerland, 1932. Page 16.
2. The word waldstaetten or waldstätten, literally means: Forest cantons. The three oldest Swiss cantons: Uri, Schwyz and Unterwalden, are called *primitive cantons.* (See Dieter Fahrni. *History of Switzerland.* Pro Helvetia, Swiss Cultural Foundation. Switzerland, 1995. Page 24).
3. The pact signed in 1291 says as follows: "The three (or four) communities *renew* under oath a previous alliance, promising to offer mutual support if they are harmed". Hence the deduction that the alliance of 1291 was not really the first one, although historically in Switzerland it is as accepted as such. (See: Pierre Cordey. *Encounter with Switzerland.* Op. Cit.)

In 1309, these cantons remained grouped under the authority of just one imperial judge, recognizing in that manner the alliance established in the year 1291.

In 1315, Duke Leopold (Habsburg), with two thousand or three thousand cavalrymen tried to recover the territories of the cantons that formed part of the pact[5], but they were repelled and crushed in Morgarten, on November 15. As a result of this victory, three weeks later, the alliance is renewed in Brunnen, drafting it this time in German (the original one had been drafted in Latin).

In 1318, an armistice is reached between the cantons that had signed the pact and the Habsburgs. The emperor confirms the privileges of the *waldstaetten.* Around the middle of the XIV century, the confederation begins to be viable, and the first links between the cities and the rural areas begin to take form.

In 1332, Lucerne affirms a perpetual alliance with the *waldstaetten,* thereby admitting the first city to that league of rural communities.

---

4. Habsburg: Germanic dynasty that originated in Suabia. Its origins go back to the X century. With Albert the Rich it conquered in 1153 part of Switzerland and Alsace. It took the imperial throne in 1273 with Rodolph of Habsburg. It reigned in Austria between 1279 and 1918 and arrived in Spain through the marriage between Phillip the Handsome (a son of Maximilian I), and Juana the Crazy One (a daughter of the Catholic Monarchs). It was known in Spain as the House of Austria. (See: Pierre Renouvin. *History of International Relations, Tome I, Volume I.* Aguilar Editorial. Spain, 1967).
5. The men taken by Duke Leopold came from Upper Germany, a territory that later became part of Switzerland. (See: Pierre Cordey, *Meeting with Switzerland.* Op. Cit.)

In 1351, Zürich, which after a revolution of the guilds feared an attempt at restoration of the nobility, also allied itself to them. Glarus and Zug did it in 1352 and 1353 respectively; on the other hand, Berne, who struggled to expand its zone of influence towards the west, joined likewise that nucleus of confederate cantons (1353).

With occasional truces, the struggle between the confederates and the Habsburgs went on. In July of 1386, near the city of Sempach, there was an encounter between the confederate forces and six thousand men of the duke of Austria; the duke died and his men were forced to flee. The name *Schwyzer* began to be heard.[6]

In 1338, the canton of Glarus, with the aid of a handful of men from the *walsdtaetten*, crushed the Austrians in Nafels; the Habsburgs had been defeated for a second time, and they were forced to sign a peace pact.

In 1393, the *Sempach Agreement* is signed, and with it the confederates once again tighten their alliance, thus establishing a type of common military law. This period is known as *period of the eight cantons*, and in reality is the beginning of the Helvetian Confederation as such. It should be mentioned here the common treaty *Pfaffenbrief,* (letter of the clergy), that helped to tighten the cohesion of the allied elements.

---

6. Schwyzer: Swiss. The German name of Switzerland (Schweiz) derives from Schwyz, and thus this canton has given its name to the country, as well as its colors, the white cross in a red background. (See: Pierre Cordey, *Meeting with Switzerland.* Op. Cit.)

By the end of the XIV century, it could be said that the confederation had already solidified, and progressively began to acquire the consistency of an independent state within the Germanic Empire.

Between 1439 and 1444 several confrontations take place among the confederate themselves, confrontations that ended with the signing of a national peace, which let the confederation give signs of vigor and at the same time, of cohesion, even though it was ruined by those struggles. During this period, the confederation increased from eight to thirteen cantons. Fribourg and Solothurn became members after the wars of Burgundy (1481); Basel and Schaffhausen, after the war of Suabia (1501) and Appenzell during the Italian wars (1513).

Thus is born what later would be known as *Confederation of the Thirteen Cantons* which is going to last almost three centuries, until the French Revolution.

In 1516, after their defeat at the hands of the King of France, the cantons signed with him a peace treaty, and afterwards an alliance that gave him the right to recruit troops in Switzerland (1521). All the cantons, (except Zürich, which abstained until the XVII century) adhered to the alliance; such an alliance constitutes a unique case in the history of Switzerland, and created the bases to establish close military and economic links with that neighboring country, links that lasted until the sinking of the former confederation.

In 1597, something happened which, in spite of its religious origins, transcended the borders of politics (although some authors ascribe to it a meaning merely symbolic); Appenzell splits into two *semi-cantons*, one Catholic and the other Protestant (Appenzell Ausserrhoden and Appenzell Innerrhoden). The effects of the Reformation and the Counter-Reformation were beginning to be felt.[7]

In December 1797, when France occupies the territory of the Bishopric of Basel in the Jura canton, the Great Council of Basel rushed to grant freedom and equal rights to the subjects of that city. The chief of the guilds, Peter Ochs (1752-1821) was a convinced supporter of the democratic renovation and as such, he induced the aristocracy to act before the storm would overtake them, carrying a revolution of their own will. The country of Vaud also had an ardent advocate of the revolution: Frederic Cesar de la Harpe

---

7. *Reform*: A European religious movement initiated in the XVI century. It meant the rupture of the unity of the Roman Catholic Church. Its main promoter was Martin Luther, who gave in Germany its theological formula regarding the Lutheran Protestantism. In the rest of Europe the other main branches of Protestantism were inspired by the Zurichan Ulrico Zwingli and John Calvin in Switzerland (Calvinism); by J. Knox in Scotland (Presbyterianism) and by Henry VIII in England (Anglicanism). The Reform had two consequences that were transcendental for Europe, not only in the religious level, but also in the social, political, economical, and ideological levels. The irreversible religious division of Europe is approved in *The Peace of Habsburg* (1555). However, terrible religious confrontations would still take place, ending in the *Thirty Years War* (1618-1648). This war came to an end with the signing of the *Peace of Westphalia*, by which Europe recognized Switzerland as a sovereign state.

   Counter-Reformation: In an effort to block the effects of the Reform, the Catholic Church created a reactionary movement to oppose the advance of Protestantism (XVI century). It initially adopted a repressive characteristic (restoration of Inquisition by Paul III). In spite of the *Trent Council* (1545-1563), it promoted a vast reform movement within the Catholic Church itself. (See: Fisher H.A.L. *History of Europe, Tome I*. Editorial Sudamericana. Argentina, 1946).

(1754-1838). The liberation of Berne and the birth of the Lemanian Republic were proclaimed before the arrival of the French troops on January 28, 1798. The Diet[8] remained undecided in view of the advance of the French army.

In the lower Valais and in the valleys south from the Alps, the subjects proclaimed themselves free; Zürich and Schaffhausen established equal rights. In Aargau and in other places, the French were received as liberators coming to end the patriarchal absolutism. Berne attempted to offer an individual resistance to the French army, but it was defeated; the ancient confederation was coming to its end. The Helvetian Revolution had triumphed, even though under the sign of a foreign domination. Napoleon proclaimed a new Constitution trying to change the confederation into a republic unique and indivisible: the Helvetian Republic.

From 1798 to 1848 there was a transition towards a Federal State, during this time (it is superfluous to mention it) several retrogressions took place. The State crisis was permanent and the conservative forces opposed the innovating forces in several occasions.

The Helvetian Republic soon was victim of internal struggles, and even five coups d'état took place between 1800 and 1802, which ended in a civil war when the Napoleonic forces moved out.

Napoleon once again rushed to occupy once again Switzerland and enacted in 1803 the *Act of Mediation* (actually a new Constitution),

---

8.   Diet: Political assembly of certain states that have formed a confederation, and in which public affairs are discussed. General Assembly of the territorial chiefs in a feudal state.

by which he returns to many cantons many of the former authorities. It also establishes again the Assembly that existed at another time. The unified republic becomes a federated republic. As the cantons began to recover their rights and autonomy, the country began to acquire certain stability in its political situation. That same year (1803), takes place the addition of the cantons of St. Gall, Graubünden (Grisones), Aargau, Thurgau, Ticino and Vaud, thus reaching a total of nineteen confederated cantons.

After Napoleon's fall, the sympathizers of the former regime in Switzerland requested a return to the former confederation, thus beginning in 1814 a process that has been known as *Restoration.* The *Vienna Congress* transformed Switzerland into a confederation of states in 1815, and recognized its neutrality. The official title *Swiss Confederation* in use nowadays, originated in those days. On that same year (1815), three new cantons joined Switzerland: Valais, Neuchâtel and Genève.

Around 1830, the liberal currents in Switzerland acquired again a new vigor, and this favored the beginning of the *regeneration,* which provoked tensions in Basel and ended up in a civil war between the city and the country in 1833; as a result, the cantons was divided in two half cantons: Basel Stadt and Basel Land.

After 1848 begins what we could well call the *Modern Switzerland.* The constituents did not want a centralized and unitary state, and for that reason they sought the economic union only. In the political field they created a federal power in which the sovereignty is shared among citizens and cantons, and which is product of its same history and tradition. A new bicameral parliament system is adopted, through which the parliamentary system is exercised. Originally they wanted an executive power subordinated to the legislative, and this, together with the national tradition made them decide for a college: The Federal Council. Thus a representative system of relations between parliament and executive is created, different from the parliament regime per se. The executive is elected both Parliament Chambers meeting in a Federal Assembly, but they cannot overthrow it. At the same time the executive cannot dissolve the chambers. The Federal Tribunal was also created based on the national tradition.

The Constitution is approved in 1848 and is totally revised in 1874; the institutions that to this time had given proof of their efficiency, were not touched, although the revision restricted the rights of the cantons and expanded the rights of the confederation and the citizens. A *legislative referendum* was introduced and the freedom of conscience was consolidated. Later on some partial revisions were carried out, which somehow came to strengthen the direct democracy (or rather partially direct): constitutional initiative (1891); strict limitations to the urgency clause (1949); feminine suffrage (1971).

In 1979, the Swiss Confederation witnessed the birth of a twenty third canton: the Jura canton, which was created as a culmination of a process that had begun in 1974, and which was the result of a conflict between the French-speaking canton of Bernes Jura and the authorities of the canton of Berne, which had come to produce (1974) a secessionist movement in that area. Thus, Switzerland arrives at the twenty-three (23) cantons that now form the Confederation.[9]

---

9.   Ibid.

2

THE REGIME OF CONVENTION

2.1. STRUCTURE OF THE REGIME OF CONVENTION

The regime of convention or conventional regime is one of the governmental structures that exist nowadays in the world (although actually not the most popular). Seen from a simplistic angle, it is based in the agreement and the stipulation of the involved parties. According to Douglas V. Verney, there are at least three different ways to organize the executive and legislative branches of government: a) *both powers may rest in the hands of a single man, an absolute monarch or a dictator;* b) *the legislative and executive functions may be separate, as they are more or less in the parliamentary government, as the presidential* and c) *there may be a combination of both functions in one assembly*[1].

Based on this last case, the focus of power in the political system we now discuss is the Assembly (supreme branch of the government). It is elected through direct suffrage and exercises, among other functions, the legislative power; it can dissolve itself, but no other entity may dissolve it.

Government, whose members are elected by the Assembly[2], exercises the executive power, and also has some interference in the governmental functions. Government is a collective organ (collegiate), politically responsible before the Assembly and only indirectly responsible to the electorate. Members of the Government in many cases are part of the Assembly.

---

1.   Douglas V. Verney, *Analysis of Political Systems.* Op. Cit.
2.   Ibid.

The judicial power is exercised by the Tribunals, which generally have jurisdiction in civil, penal, administrative, and public right matters, as well as others, but they do not enjoy competence in matters of constitutionality (the Swiss case). Its members are *appointed* by the Assembly.[3]

---

3.   Ibid.

2.2. THE SWISS FEDERALISM

In the context of the political institutions in Switzerland (and for a better understanding of them), *Federalism* cannot be overlooked. In Switzerland, Federalism is seen as a *union without rigidity* by the cantons that form the Confederation. The centers of political decision, and therefore the power and the duties of the State, are distributed. The cantons enjoy some sovereignty and even have their own municipal constitutions[4] as well as their own political organs, such as governments, parliaments[5] and local tribunals.

The quality as a state of the cantons is appropriate in matters of police, indigence, education and cultural matters, while the Confederation is responsible for foreign policy, custom houses, post offices, etc. In other numerous areas, such as fiscal policy, transportation, social matters and energy, a growing transfer is seen of the competences of the Federation, which change the cantons into executive organizations.

On the other hand, the economic development, the unification of the law and its orientation in international matters, as well as the noticeable evolution of the public finances (especially in the last lustrums), have reinforced also in Switzerland the centralizing trends.

---

4.   See: Articles 5, 6, 85, and 102 of the Federal Constitution of the Swiss Confederation.

5.   The parliament cantons (different from the federal parliament, which is bicameral) are unicameral, and the number of their members, as well as the length of their functioning periods, may vary according to each canton. The canton government (executive canton) has 5, 7 or 9 members, who function according to the collegiate system. Both parliament and local government are elected by secret scrutiny of the electoral votes (with the exception of cantons with *Landsgemeinde*). (See: Kummerly + Frey. *Switzerland.* Switzerland, 1998. Page 34).

This transfer of competences that takes place nowadays, is called *executive federalism*. It is also important to mention, however, the called *cooperative federalism*, which consists in the realization of municipal efforts whose purpose is to solve problems between cantons without federal intervention; as a matter of fact, the Federal Constitution establishes the *inter-canton concordat*, defined as an agreement signed among the cantons regarding legislation, administration, or justice matters, in which the federal authority may *cooperate* for its execution.[6]

Should be there any opposition from any of the cantons, the Federal Constitution establishes the steps that have to be followed.[7]

---

6. See: Pier Felice Barchi. *Meeting Switzerland—The Political Institutions.* OSEC. Switzerland, 1982. Page 132
7. See: Article 7, article 85, clause 5; article 110, clause 3; article 113, clauses 2 and 3; Federal Constitution of the Swiss Confederation.

2.3. THE SWISS FEDERAL ASSEMBLY

The exercise of the legislative power is one of the main tasks of the Federal Assembly, task that carries out with parliamentarian initiatives, motions and postulates[8].

Parliament is bicameral: *The National Council* which nowadays is formed by two hundred (200) members (representing the totality of the Swiss population) and *The States Council* made up of forty six (46) congressmen (representing cantons). Both Cameras enjoy the same rights and deal with the same matters.

Parliament *elects* members of the Federal Council (Government) and *appoints* members of the Federal Tribunal[9] and has authority to intervene against the Government, forcing it to offer account of all type of questions, through interpellations or simple questions presented orally or in writing.

---

8.   *Motion*: It is an independent petition that tends to force the Federal Council (executive) to submit a project of a bill or decree, or gives instructions related to a measure that must be taken, or to proposals that must be made. A motion accepted by one of the Chambers will acquire features of imperative instruction to the Federal Council only when the Chamber approves it. *The Postulate*: It is an independent petition through which an invitation is extended to the Federal Council to determine if a project of a bill or decree should be presented, or if certain measure should be adopted. (See: Kummerly + Frey. *Switzerland*. Op. Cit. Page 37).

9.   In the election of members to the Federal Council, or also in cases of amnesties, both Chambers take part in joint session, forming the Federal Assembly. Candidates to the Federal Council and the Federal Tribunal are usually proposed by the political parties. (See: Oswald Sigg. *Politics in Switzerland*. Pro Helvetia, Swiss Cultural Foundation. Switzerland, 1995. Page 36).

Parliament does not have as a function to give vote of confidence or lack of it to the Government, although both Chambers exercise a true function of executive control through the permanent commissions. Besides, the Assembly has competence in matters of *financial balances* of the Confederation; it approves the budget and the State accounts.

Parliament meets in four periods of sessions during the year, each session lasts three weeks, and during that time it works through *commissions,* which prepare debates in general sessions of the National Council and the States Council. The commissions may be permanent, or be ad hoc commissions formed to consider special projects.

The most important permanent commissions nowadays are:

- Financial commissions (of the National Council and the States Council)

- Auditing commissions

- Foreign policy commissions

- Commissions for science and formation of culture

- Commissions for social security and health

- Commissions for the environment, territorial conditioning and energy

- Commissions for political safety

- Commissions for transportation and telecommunications

"Parliament performs the most important role in the beginning of a law. However, the momentum for a new law may come from outside both Chambers, be it at the request of the cantons, of the diverse political parties, or in the case of an article of the Constitution, by popular initiative. The organs of social communication are sometimes indirectly involved in the initiation of an initiative.

The Federal Council receives an idea and delegates in its administration the preparation of a project of law (new article in the Constitution or a new federal law) as the case may be, but after consultation with external experts. This project then goes through the process known as adoption of position, in which the cantons, the associations, the political parties and other interested institutions are consulted, and then are invited to formulate their judgment about the project. Only after this process there is a project of law refined and ready to be promulgated by the Federal Council. The next step is to present the project to the Parliament, together with the so-called message (explanatory report), after which both Chambers, acting separately, begin the corresponding deliberation, preparing it to present it to the competent commissions.[10]

After the final voting at the National Council and the Council of States, the Federal Council, should it be obligatory to do so, will set a date for a voting by the people and the States (cantons). After receiving a decision by the Parliament, a new law is published in the *Federal Sheet*, organism of official publication. If within the following three months after that publication the referendum with at least fifty thousand (50,000) is not asked for, the federal law becomes

---

10.   Oswald Sigg. *Politics in Switzerland.* Op. Cit.

effective; otherwise, the law becomes effective only if it is approved through a referendum.

Regarding the form of election of the National Council, (which has two hundred (200) benches in proportion with the population of the cantons), the representatives are elected by the proportional system, in which each canton is an electoral circumscription, and not when the country is a single circumscription.

The manner of election of the representatives before the Council of States (46 benches, corresponding two to each canton, and one to each semi-canton)[11], is by the authority of each canton. Long time ago, some cantons elected them through a local parliament; nowadays all cantons do it directly through a popular vote.[12]

---

11. Two seats belong to the Council of the States in each canton. Since three cantons exist which are subdivided in semi-cantons of half cantons, only half a seat corresponds to each half canton, thereby keeping a total of 46 seats. (See Articles 72 and 80 of the Federal Constitution of the Swiss Confederation).
12. See: Articles 71 through 94 of the Federal Constitution of the Swiss Confederation.

2.4. THE SWISS FEDERAL COUNCIL

The right to exercise the executive power falls on the Federal Council (Swiss Government), which is elected every four years by the Federal Assembly.[13] It is composed of six members and it is led by one of them (President of the Confederation), elected each time for a one year period.

The president of the Confederation conducts the sessions of the Federal Council and assumes the duties of representing the State; but at the same time continues acting as a minister, remaining at the head of his department (secretariat).

The Swiss government is divided in seven main departments or secretariats, which in turn are led by one member of the Federal Council (federal advisers). The federal advisers lead administrative complexes, which would usually correspond to several secretariats in other countries.

The Federal Council is composed of members of several parties, a heterogeneous composition that becomes a feature typically Swiss and corresponds to the political system of concordance and collegiality. There is a union in the Government of the political forces that predominate in both Chambers (Parliament) and which in part are divergent.

---

13. The election is carried out by both Chambers, which meet in joint session in the room of the National Council. (See: Chapter II, Federal Constitution of the Swiss Confederation).

A member of the Federal Council may resign on his own initiative, but he cannot be expelled or forced to resign. Parliament cannot force Government or any of its members to resign.

2.4.1. The Federal Chancellery

The Federal Chancellery acts as a secretariat of the Government; it is led by a Federal Chancellor and has available central juridical services, linguistic services, services of the central printing press, central information services, as well as control of its administration.

The most important task of the Federal Chancellery is informing the population about referendums and government matters. One of the two Vice-chancellors acts as a spokesperson for the Government. Both Federal Chancellor and Federal Council are elected by the Federal Assembly for a four-year period...*the Chancellery is under the special control of the Federal Council...a federal law shall determine matters referring to the organization of the Chancellery...*[14]

2.4.2. Current departments of the Swiss Government and their main responsibilities

—*Federal Department of Foreign Matters* (DFAE): Foreign policy, diplomatic and consular representations, peace policy, security and disarmament, relations with the European Union and with international organizations, cooperation for humanitarian development and assistance.

---

14.   Article 105, Chapter II, Title III, Federal Constitution of the Swiss Confederation.

—*Federal Department of the Interior* (DFI): Culture, federal constructions, health, environment, statistics, social security, science and investigation and sports.

—*Federal Department of Justice and Police* (DFJP): Justice, police, aliens matters, Secretariat of Interior for the Confederation, private security, intellectual rights, civil protection, development of the natural resources, cadastral measurements, exiles.

—*Federal Department of Defense, Protection of the Population and Sports* (DFDPD): Sports, policy of security and defense.

—*Federal Department of Finances* (DFF): Federal Finances, federal personal, warehouses, federal taxes, informatics, vigilance of banks.

—*Federal Department of Public Economy* (DFEP): Exterior economy, industry, commerce and work, agriculture, matters with the economy, defense of the economy, housing.

—*Federal Department of Transportation, Communication and Energy* (DFTCE): Highway, railroad and air transportation, energy, highways building, communications and telecommunications, federal railroads, mail, telegraph and telephones.

2.5. THE SWISS FEDERAL TRIBUNAL

Contrary to the Parliament and the Government, which have their headquarters in Berne, the Federal Tribunal is located in Laussane, a city at Lake Leman, city selected in 1874 for that purpose.

The Federal Tribunal nowadays is formed by thirty (30) judges (of both sexes) and also by fifteen (15) substituting judges appointed by the Federal Assembly for a period of six years. The candidates running for these positions are usually presented by the political parties.

The Swiss Supreme Tribunal is divided in eight offices in charge of civil, penal, administrative cases and public law, as well as matters that arise between the Confederation and the cantons[15]. Regarding matters related to constitutional articles or texts of law, the Federal Tribunal lacks jurisdiction, therefore, it does not pass judgment on those matters due to its lack of constitutionality. The last word in State matters is emitted only to the people through a mechanism such as the referendum.

As part of the judicial system, although it is also connected to the Federal Department of the Interior, mention should be made of the Federal Tribunal of Insurances, with headquarters in Lucerne, whose main function is to pass judgment on complaints and on social security matters.

---

15.   *...the cantons have the right, subject to approbation by the Federal Assembly, to know about the administrative differences in canton matters...*(Article 114 bis, of the Federal Constitution of the Swiss Confederation).

3

SOMETHING ABOUT…

3.1. MUNICIPAL AUTONOMY

The canton is a corporation of public right that acts on its territory with a decentralized power by means of its own administration. The political canton is found in all cantons. [1]

The 3018 communes existing nowadays have (same as the cantons and the Confederation) a local government that usually is called *municipal council* and with a *local assembly or neighbors committee* (local parliament). [2] These are entities that make decisions and carry out elections. In these cities, those local parliaments are replaced by means of written elections and voting.

The canton deals, in the first place, with matters related to municipal finances (obligatory type, canton's budget, etc.). It also takes decisions regarding elementary and secondary schools, police norms and municipal safety (fire, water), cemeteries, urbanizing, sport and cultural activities, environment, and others.

The public services are most of them usually rendered by the canton through its municipal employees, although in many cases are provided by private companies hired for that purpose.

---

1.   In some cantons the municipality is called *community of neighbors.*
2.   In some cantons the municipal council is called *Town hall or Borough Council.*

3.2. The Landsgemeinden

Landsgemeinden literally means *municipal community*, and it goes back to the times of the foundation of the old confederation.

In the rural cantons of Obwalden, Nidwalden and Glarus, the Swiss direct democracy is still practiced in a primitive way: the Landsgemeinden. This is an assembly of citizens with the *right to voting*, that meets in order to decide political matters.

In this case, however, when speaking about the right to vote, one refers to something relative, since each canton with Landsgemeindens establishes its own municipal constitution, its mechanisms, procedures and rights in its own jurisdiction regarding this topic. At federal level, the right to vote is acquired nowadays after the citizen reaches 18 years of age (men and women) whereas previously the age was 20 years and women were not allowed to vote.[3]

This people's assembly, one that votes and elects, usually meets twice a year at the central plaza of the capital city in each canton. Each citizen (man or woman) may speak in order to deal with any matter in order to influence the voting, which normally is public.[4]

In the cantons of Schwyz and Zug, Landsgemeinden stopped being held in 1848; in Uri, it was observed until 1928-1929; and in Appenzell Ausserrhoden it was abolished in 1997.[5]

---

3. It should be emphasized that this happens only in the case of Landsgemeinde.
4. Ibid.

3.3. DIRECT DEMOCRACY

Direct democracy is of great importance within the political system of Switzerland. It is necessary to point out in first place, the *referendum* (officially denominated obligatory referendum) through which the Swiss people could express itself in favor or against changes or reforms to the Federal Constitution.

The federal laws may also be approved or rejected (whatever the case may be) by people's verdict, through the *optional referendum.*

When Parliament promulgates a federal law that could find opposition from certain group, association, political party, etc., there is a period of ninety (90) days during which, those citizens (men or women) who are in disagreement with said law, may request the Federal Chancellery, through fifty thousand (50,000) signatures, that the law be submitted for popular consultation. If such a petition is not presented, the law becomes effective at the end of the 90 days.[6]

Probably the most important political party of the Swiss people, however, could well be that of the *popular initiative*[7] which is the

---

5. A considerable number of districts in Graubünden (Grisones) know nowadays the Landsgemeinden, but the topics discussed there limit themselves mainly to appointment of judicial authorities and the deputies of the local parliament, or members of the local government. It should be mentioned here the figure of the *Landammann,* name given to the individual that performs official functions in the canton, and who in many instances is also judge, chief of State, and president of the Landsgemeinden. (See: Dieter Fahrni. *History of Switzerland.* Op. Cit).

6. In this case, people can only lean in favor or against a bill and not in favor of an alternative. (See: Articles 89 and 89 bis of the Federal Constitution of the Swiss Confederation).

possibility that one hundred thousand (100,000) citizens (men and women) with the right to vote, collect signatures in a period of one and one half years and present them to the Federal Chancellery, asking that a new constitutional article be adopted, or that an article of the Federal Constitution be repealed, or be modified. Nevertheless, one of the greatest inconveniences of this important right is its slowness, because the process goes from the introduction of a new popular initiative, until the popular voting, and this could easily last up to five years, after which the political importance of the question stops being important.

The process includes: collection of signatures, preparation of the project, decision by the federal administration[8], decision about an initiative, scheduling a date for voting, and popular voting itself.

Additionally, there also exists the right to *petition,* which is done in writing and addressed to the proper authorities. Each citizen (man or woman), whatever his or her voting capability, may sign it, and for that this petition has an uncertain effect. The addressees (proper authorities), be it the Federal Council or one of the Chambers of the Federal Assembly, only have the obligation to accept the petition.

---

7.   Nowadays, due to a long and complicated process, the right to *popular initiative* seems to have remained more as an important right in the constitutional theory, and with a minor importance in practice.

8.   The Government and the Parliament cannot intervene directly against it, but are able to simultaneously present a counterproposal, and see that it is voted one way or another. However, they cannot modify the text of the bill. (See Chapter III, *Reform of the Federal Constitution.* Federal Constitution of the Swiss Confederation).

Different from the referendum and the initiative, this petition cannot be considered an obligation[9].

---

9.   As a rule, petitions are indicators of the popular movements, and their contents sometimes are object of popular initiatives. (See: Articles 89; 89 bis; 120; 121;122; and 123 of the Federal Constitution of the Swiss Confederation).

4

SWITZERLAND TODAY

4.1. IN THE MANNER OF A CONCLUSION

Since the foundation of the Swiss Confederation in 1291, known then with the name of *Perpetual League*, the union conformed by the cantons of Uri, Schwyz and Unterwalden, evolved to become (already with 22 cantons) from a confederation of states to a federal state[1].

The Constitution adopted in 1848 granted the cantons certain sovereignty and autonomy, but as it was logical, transferred to the Confederation the functions and assignments due to a national State. However, in spite of the sovereignty and autonomy already planned at a municipal level, the Constitution was new regarding the implementation of bases to arrive to the real exercise of a direct democracy (or semi-direct) which is what the Swiss people enjoys currently.

In 1874 and 1891, some revisions were made to the Constitution, which brought about the introduction of the *facultative referendum and the popular initiative*, with which the Swiss had in their hands tools for a direct democracy, tools through which they are able nowadays to tackle and regulate questions or political matters, including at the level of the Constitution itself[2].

---

1.   Currently the Swiss Confederation consists of 23 cantons, but just only the Jura Canton was integrated in the XX century (in 1979).
2.   For a long time, nothing was said about women's political rights. As an example we could mention how in Appenzell Ausserrhoden, women could attend for the first time a Landsgemeinden in 1990 (abolished in said canton in 1997). The Federal Tribunal also granted in 1990 the right for women to vote in their cantons in Appenzell Innerrhoden. (See: Federal Constitution of the Swiss Confederation).

The direct democracy (as it has been mentioned before), is of utter importance to the political system in Switzerland, and it is not an exaggeration to say that it is, to a great extent, the origin of what now is known as Swiss Confederation. Nevertheless, when mention is made of the Helvetian Confederation and the system of agreement that characterizes it, it becomes necessary to set up certain characteristics of the convention regime, which could be points of reference and a recapitulation regarding the main theories of government existing nowadays.

The regimen of convention (or conventional) is a government system that is based mainly in the concordance (already referred to) and in the agreements. Members of the majority of the political institutions (especially at a federal level) are appointed or elected by a superior entity, which to a great extent monopolizes both the legislative and the executive branches.

In the particular case of Switzerland, the Federal Assembly (National Council and States Council), are elected by the people through direct suffrage; at the same time, this Assembly elects or appoints (as the case may be) the members of said Assembly and the candidate proposed by the respective political parties.

These characteristics, among others, make the Swiss political system an important part in the context of government theories. On the other hand, the political parties, the associations and the social media perform a very singular role in the Helvetian political system, constituting fundamental elements in the Swiss political activities.

At a municipal level, the political parties are consulted by the authorities in matters related to aspects which, at any given time, may affect or involve the people. As an example we could mention the appointment to public positions, the make up of school commissions, etc., matters in which the political parties have the last word. The associations, however, and given their larger economic capacity and their better infrastructure, enjoy a position slightly stronger than that of the parties, achieving in this manner an important influence in the political happenings of the Confederation. The unions and the businessmen are nowadays the main actors in the area of associations. This type of organizations may exert their influence even at a federal level.

On the other hand, the function of the social media cannot avoid being controversial, because apart from the classical role of the *fourth estate*, which consists in the vigilance of the exercise of power by the political parties (Parliament, Government, and Justice), grants the commented publication of the political activities, more than can be found in other countries.

All this unavoidably takes us to raise the following question: Does Switzerland nowadays agrees with the interests and the exercise of power (as a block) in the rest of the European continent? Within the frame of the European integration, and due to the legislative system in (and the government of) Switzerland, not counting on its traditional neutralism, foreign policy, autarchy, etc., its *"incorporation"* to the European Community evidently *"takes place"* in a clear form and at a totally different rhythm than the rest of the nations that form it, because thought it has not really incorporated, it does cooperate with the EU in several fields, such as environment, marketing, and development[3].

Fully integration to the European Union would also signify a transformation of the political institutions which according to some Swiss citizens (men and women), would give as a result a loss of sovereignty, something they do not seem to be willing to accept.

In this sense, and with basis on what has been said about the conventional theory carried out in practice as a form of government, makes it possible that it may be better to analyze the Swiss political system in its practice, and not in its form.

---

3.   See: Paul Keller. *Economic life and export industries.* Swiss Office of Commercial Expansion. Switzerland, 1982. Pages 24-28.

5

APENDIX I

5.1. A Profile of Switzerland

Geologically speaking, Switzerland is a complex country. It is part of the Alpine arc, which spans over almost 1,000 kilometers between Nice (French maritime Alps) and Vienna (Austrian Alps). The southern borders of the country penetrate at the south the Italian plains and at the north, past Rhine river, the Black Forest.

Three main natural regions are considered to integrate the Swiss territory: Alps and Pre-Alps (60%), Plains (30%) and Jura (10%).

Switzerland covers the central part of the Alps, and this is equivalent to one fifth of its total territorial extension. The longitudinal valleys of Rodano and the Upper Rhine, as well as the lateral valleys of Reuss and Ticino, subdivide the bulk of mountains in an eastern chain (Alps of Thurgau, of Glarus, of Schwyz and the eastern Alps of Uri), a western chain (Western Alps of Uri, Bernian Alps, as well as Fribourgian and Vadoisan Alps) and a southern chain (Valaisian Alps, Tecinese Alps and the Graubünden—Grisones—).

The median altitude of the Alps is in the area of 1,700 meters, while about one hundred peaks approach or overpass the 4,000 meters mark. The highest point, Point Dufour (Mountainous bulk of Monte Rosa, Alps of Valais) reaches 4,634 meters. The Pre-Alps, in the northwestern slope of the Alps, comprised mostly of conglomerates, offer a less complex structure, and its highest points approach 2,000 meters.

The plains area has an average altitude of 580 meters. The area is a curved wide strip that runs between Lake Leman and Lake Constanza, with a climate less severe than the Alps or the Jura. Between these two chains there is a corridor (the plains) where the population and means of communication, agriculture and industry concentrate.

On the other hand, the Jura is an arc of rugged slopes, valleys and tablelands of a simpler general structure than that of the Alps. It has an average altitude of 700 meters, although some of the peaks reach 1,600 meters (Mont Tendré/Vaud: 1,679 meters). It shows itself in three parts: Jura to the south, Jura of the tablelands, and a tabular Jura at north and at east.

Politically, Switzerland is organized as a states confederation (cantons)[1], whose total surface is 41,293 square kilometers; located at the heart of Europe (between 45 and 47 degrees latitude north and between 5 and 11 degrees longitude east). It has common borders at north with Germany, west with France, south with Italy, east with Austria, Liechtenstein and Italy. It is conformed by the cantons of Aargau, Appenzell Ausserrhoden, Appenzell Innerrhoden, Basel—Stadt, Basel Land, Berne[2], Fribourg, Geneva, Glarus, Graubünden (Grisons), Jura, Lucerne, Neuchâtel, Nidwalden, Obwalden, Schaffhausen, Schwyz, Solothurn, St. Gallen, Thurgau, Ticino, Uri, Valais, Vaud, Zug and Zürich.

---

1. The Swiss Confederation consists of 23 cantons, although three of them are subdivided in half cantons: Appenzell: Ausserrhoden and Innerrhoden; Basel: Stadt and Land; Unterwalden: Obwalden and Nidwalden. Unterwalden was divided between the XII and XIV centuries. Appenzell was divided in 1597. Basel was divided in 1833.
2. Berne is the capital of the Swiss Confederation.

Its government system is based (as it has been seen) in the *regime of convention or conventional regime*; its currency is the Swiss franc[3] and its national languages are German, French, Italian, and Romanche or Rhaeto-Romanic[4] although there are other Franco-Provencal and Lombard languages, as well as Bernese, Zuriques, Bales, etc., which are spoken by minorities in determined sectors of the Confederation[5].

Its total population surpassed 3.3 million inhabitants (1900) to 6.7 million (1991), and a growth was estimated for the year 2000 to 6.83 million, but due to a decrease in the birth rate and an increase in life expectancy, the Swiss population presents nowadays a clear trend towards aging. At the end of 2001 (December) its total population was 7 million 261,210 (Swiss's and immigrants), 0.8% more than 2000 (5 million 834,100 Swiss's and 1 million 486,800 immigrants).[6]

---

3. One Swiss franc is divided into one hundred cents. Bills currently in circulation are 10, 20, 50, 100, 500 and 1000 francs. Coins are 5, 10, 20, and 50 cents, 1, 2, and 5 francs.

4. Rhaeto-Romanic: Language of Latin origin, spoken (besides in Switzerland) in northern Italy.

5. Article 116 of the Federal Constitution of the Swiss Confederation establishes like *national languages* German, French, Italian, and Rhaeto-Romanic; but makes it clear that the *official languages of the Confederation* are only German, French, and Italian. The remaining existing dialects are not recognized as *official* at the federal level.

6. Data obtained from information and graphs published by OSEC in: How to Export to Switzerland, 1991; and www.statik.admin.ch (2002).

6

APENDIX II

6.1. THE CANTONS (STATES)

—**Aargau (AG):** Capital: *Aarau.* Territory size: 1,404 square kilometers. Population: 423,000 inhabitants. Administrative language: German. Member of Swiss Confederation since 1,803.

—**Appenzell Ausserhoden (AR):** Capital: *Herisau.* Territory size: 243 square kilometers. Population: 50,900. Administrative language: German. Member of Swiss Confederation since: 1,513.

—**Appenzell Innerrhoden (AL):** Capital: *Appenzell City (Appenzell).* Territory size: 174 square kilometers. Population: 13,500 inhabitants. Administrative language: German. Member of Swiss Confederation since: 1,513.

—**Basel-Stadt (BS):** Capital: *Basel City (Stadt Basel).* Territory size: 36 square kilometers. Population: 190,300 inhabitants. Administrative language: German. Member of Swiss Confederation since: 1,501.

—**Basel-Landschaft (BL):** Capital: *Liestal.* Territory size: 427 square kilometers. Population: 229,000 inhabitants. Administrative language: German. Member of Swiss Confederation since: 1,501.

—**Berne (BE):** Capital: *Bern City (Bern/Berne Ville).* Territory size: 6,883 square kilometers. Population: 939,000 inhabitants. Administrative languages: German and French. Member of Swiss Confederation since: 1,353.

—**Fribourg (FR):** Capital: *Fribourg City (Freiburg/Ville Fribourg).* Territory size: 1,671 square kilometers. Population: 279,000 inhabitants. Administrative languages: French and German. Member of Swiss Confederation since: 1,481

—**Geneva (GE):** Capital: *Geneva City (Ville de Genève).* Territory size: 282 square kilometers. Population: 373,000 inhabitants. Administrative language: French. Member of Swiss Confederation since: 1,815.

—**Glarus (GL):** Capital: *Glarus City (Stadt Glarus).* Territory size: 684 square kilometers. Population: 37,000 inhabitants. Administrative language: German. Member of Swiss Confederation since: 1,352.

—**Grisons (GR):** Capital: *Chur.* Territory size: 7,105 square kilometers. Population: 373,000 inhabitants. Administrative language: German. Member of Swiss Confederation since: 1,803.

—**Jura (JU):** Capital: *Delemont.* Territory size: 840 square kilometers. Population: 64,900 inhabitants. Administrative language: French. Member of Swiss Confederation since: 1,978.

—**Lucerne (LU):** Capital: *Lucerne (Luzern City/Stadt Luzern).* Territory size: 1,492 square kilometers. Population: 314,800 inhabitants. Administrative language: German. Member of Swiss Confederation since: 1,332.

—**Neuchâtel (NE):** Capital: *Neuchâtel City (Ville Neuchâtel).* Territory size: 800 square kilometers. Population: 159,000 inhabitants. Administrative language: French. Member of Swiss Confederation since: 1,815.

—**Nidwalden (NW):** Capital: *Stans*. Territory size: 275 square kilometers. Population: 32,000 inhabitants. Administrative language: German. Member of Swiss Confederation since: 1,291.

—**Obwalden (OW):** Capital: *Sarnen*. Territory size: 492 square kilometers. Population: 28,300 inhabitants. Administrative language: German. Member of Swiss Confederation since: 1,291.

—**Schaffhausen (SH):** Capital: *Schaffhausen City (Stadt Schaffhausen)*. Territory size: 298 square kilometers. Population: 71,000 inhabitants. Administrative language: German. Member of Swiss Confederation since: 1,501.

—**Schwyz (SZ):** Capital: *Schwyz City (Stadt Schwyz)*. Territory size: 909 square kilometers. Population: 108,000 inhabitants. Administrative language: German. Member of Swiss Confederation since: 1,291.

—**Solothurn (SO):** Capital: *Solothurn City (Stadt Solothurn)*. Territory size: 791 square kilometers. Population: 220,000 inhabitants. Administrative language: German. Member of Swiss Confederation since: 1,481.

—**St. Gallen (SG):** Capital: *St. Gallen City (Stadt Sankt Gallen)*. Territory size: 2,012 square kilometers. Population: 414,700 inhabitants. Administrative language: German. Member of Swiss Confederation since: 1,803.

—**Thurgau (TG):** Capital: *Frauenfeld*. Territory size: 1,005 square kilometers. Population: 201,500 inhabitants. Administrative language: German. Member of Swiss Confederation since: 1,803.

—**Ticino (TI):** Capital: *Bellinzona.* Territory size: 2,813 square kilometers. Population: 283,000 inhabitants. Administrative language: Italian. Member of Swiss Confederation since: 1,803.

—**Uri (UR):** Capital: *Altdorf.* Territory size: 1,075 square kilometers. Population: 33,500 inhabitants. Administrative language: German. Member of Swiss Confederation since: 1,291.

—**Valais (VS):** Capital: *Sion/Sitten.* Territory size: 5,234 square kilometers. Population: 243,000 inhabitants. Administrative language: German and French. Member of Swiss Confederation since: 1,815.

—**Vaud (VD):** Capital: *Lausanne.* Territory size: 3,209 square kilometers. Population: 571,000 inhabitants. Administrative language: French. Member of Swiss Confederation since: 1,803.

—**Zug (ZG):** Capital: *Zug City (Stadt Zug).* Territory size: 241 square kilometers. Population: 84,000 inhabitants. Administrative language: German. Member of Swiss Confederation since: 1,352.

—**Zürich (ZH):** Capital: *Zürich City (Stadt Zürich).* Territory size: 1,730 square kilometers. Population: 1,145,000 inhabitants. Administrative language: German. Member of Swiss Confederation since: 1,351.

BIBLIOGRAPHY

BARCHI, PIER FELICE. *Meeting Switzerland. Political Institutions.* Swiss Office for Commercial Expansion. Lausanne, Switzerland, 1982.

BOBBIO, NORBERTO. *State, Government and Society.* Fondo de Cultura Económica, México, 1989.

BOBBIO, NORBERTO. Et. Al. *Dictionary of Political Science.* Siglo Veintiuno Editores, S.A. Spain, 2001.

BORJA, RODRIGO. *Encyclopedia of Politics.* Fondo de Cultura Económica, México, 1997.

CABANELLAS DE TORRES, GUILLERMO. *Military Dictionary (aeronautical, naval, and terrestrial), Volume III.* Bibliografica Ameba. Argentina, 1963.

FEDERAL CONSTITUTION OF THE SWISS CONFEDERATION. From May 29 of 1874, with the intervening modifications until January 1, 1981; and updating until February 28, 1993.

CORDEY, PIERRY. *Meeting Switzerland. Historical Evolution.* Swiss Office for Commercial Expansion. Lausanne, Switzerland, 1982.

VERNEY, DOUGLAS V. *Analysis of Political Systems.* Tecnos Editorial, S.A.

DUVERGER, MAURICE. *Political Institutions and Constitutional Law.* Ediciones Ariel. Spain, 1970.

EVANS, GRAHAM, Et. Al. *Dictionary of International Relations.*

FAHRNI, DIETER. *History of Switzerland.* Pro Helvetia, Swiss Foundation for Culture. Switzerland, 1995.

FISHER, H.A.L. *History of Europe, Volume I.* Editorial Sudamericana. Argentina, 1946.

GARZARO, RAFAEL *Dictionary of Politics.* Cervantes Bookstore, Salamanca, Spain, 1987.

JOHNSON, HARRY. *Structure and Functioning of the Social Systems.* Paidos Editorial. Argentina, 1973

KELLER, PAUL. *Economic Life and Export Industries.* Swiss Office of Commercial Expansion. Switzerland, 1982.

KUMMERLY+FREY. *Switzerland.* Kummerly+Frey Geographic Editions. Switzerland, 1998.

LIPSON, LESLIE. *Great Problems of Politics.* Editorial Limusa—Wiley, S.A. México, 1964.

MENENDEZ PIDAL, RAMON (Publication's sponsor) *Great World Encyclopedia, Volume XVII,* Durvan, S.A. Spain, 1979.

NEWMAN, BERNARD. *The New Europe.* Fondo de Cultura Económica. México, 1944.

OSEC. *Switzerland: Basic Data. How Export to Switzerland.* Swiss Office for Promotion of Trade. Switzerland, 1991.

PIRENNE, HENRI. *History of Europe, From the XVI Century Invasions.* Fondo de Cultura Económica. México, 1942.

PORRUA, PEREZ FRANCISCO. *Theory of the State.* Editorial Porrua, S.A. México, 1971.

RENOUVIN, PIERRE. *History of International Relations, Tome I, Volume I.* Editorial Aguilar. Spain. 1967.

SERRA ROJAS, ANDRES. *Dictionary of Political Sciences (2 tomes).* Fondo de Cultura Económica. México. 1995.

SIGG, OSWALD. *Politics in Switzerland.* Pro Helvetia. Foundation for Culture. Switzerland. 1998.

STAMMEN, THEO. *Current Political Systems.* Ediciones Guadarrama. Spain. 1974.

WEISS, HANS. *Meeting Switzerland. The Landscape.* Swiss Office for Trade Expansion. Lausanne, Switzerland. 1983.

0-595-34783-5